6-8

W9-BBC-384

361.7   Rothkopf, Carol
R   Zeman.

C.1   The Red Cross

DATE			

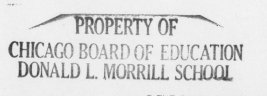

The Red Cross

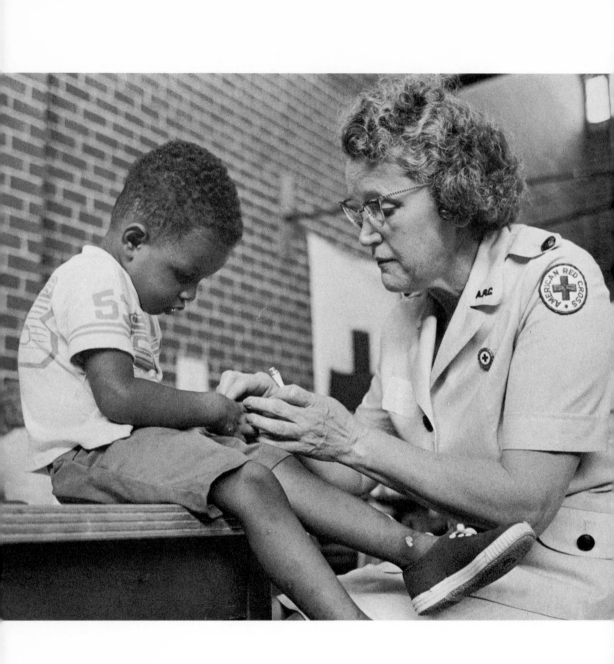

The Red Cross

by Carol Z. Rothkopf

illustrated with photographs

←A FIRST BOOK→

Franklin Watts, Inc.
845 Third Avenue
New York, N.Y. 10022

For Simonetta, Sandro, and Stefano

The photographs in this book were provided through the courtesy of the League of Red Cross Societies, Geneva, and The American National Red Cross.

SBN 531-00736-7
Copyright © 1971 by Franklin Watts, Inc.
Library of Congress Catalog Card Number: 70-134498
Printed in the United States of America

3   4   5   6

Contents

The Red Cross

The Battle of Solferino.

An Idea Is Born

Many years ago a young man arrived at a battle just as two powerful armies ended a bloody combat. The man heard the terrible cries of the wounded who lay scattered like leaves on a gray fall day.

The doctors and ambulances of the defeated army had been captured or had fled. The victorious army had only a few doctors and a small supply of medicines to care for many thousands of men. As the smoke and dust of the battle settled, a few people from a nearby village came to the battlefield to help the wounded. The man who had watched the battle helped, too. Slowly the wounded were moved to churches, private homes, and other sheltered places in the nearby town. And still the young man stayed on. For eight days he worked to feed, bandage, and comfort the soldiers. He organized the work of the volunteers and made it go more smoothly. He bought bandages, tea, lemons, cigarettes, and countless other things to make the men more comfortable. He wrote to the people in his hometown asking for their help. He argued with generals for the release of captured doctors whose help was needed. The man stopped only when exhaustion defeated him.

The terror and pain of those days never left the young man's mind. He neglected his business and even his beloved family. Finally the man wrote a book about what he had seen and learned in the hours and days after the battle. The book, *A Memory of Solferino*, was read by kings and queens, princes and prime ministers,

Jean Henri Dunant, the father of the Red Cross.

schoolteachers and priests, doctors and surgeons. Almost everyone seemed to be reading the book. And everyone was aware at last that permanent steps must be taken to end the needless suffering of the wounded in wartime. If men were not ready to end war, at least they could try to ease the pain it caused.

The result of Jean Henri Dunant's tour of the battlefield was the establishment of the International Red Cross. Today it is the world's oldest and largest charitable organization. Jean Henri Dunant (1828–1910) is honored everywhere as the father of the Red Cross.

What Is the Red Cross?

In 1863, a year after *A Memory of Solferino* was published, the Society of Public Utility in Geneva, Switzerland — Dunant's home-town — took action. A committee of five men was appointed to discuss how wounded soldiers could be helped by a permanent charitable organization. The result was the formation of the International and Permanent Committee for Relief of Wounded Soldiers, the forerunner of the International Committee of the Red Cross. In 1864 the representatives of twelve nations signed the First Geneva Convention to help soldiers wounded with "armies in the field."

The Red Cross services grew very quickly to include people other than soldiers. Today the Red Cross conventions protect sailors, prisoners of war, and civilians caught up in an international conflict. When a natural disaster such as a flood, fire, hurricane, or earthquake strikes anywhere in the world, the Red Cross provides relief services to the victims. In some countries the Red Cross owns and operates hospitals, trains nurses, and provides ambulance service. The collection, processing, and distribution of blood for emergency use is another important part of Red Cross activities in many lands. Special programs in health and hygiene have been established for some of the newer national Red Cross societies in Asia and Africa. The Red Cross also helps to teach people how to live safely, swim safely, and boat safely.

A painting of the signing ceremony for the First Geneva Convention, August 22, 1864.

More than 200,000,000 people in over one hundred countries belong to the Red Cross. Each Red Cross member nation has its own national society. The symbol for most of these organizations is a red cross on a field of white. However, in almost all Muslim countries, the symbol is a red crescent moon, and the organization that provides Red Cross services is called the Red Crescent. In Iran the society is called the Red Lion and Sun Society, and the symbol is made up of a red lion and sun.

Each national Red Cross society can develop a program of activities that is best suited to its own needs. No two societies are completely alike. But each one of the national societies is responsible to act for its government in carrying out the provisions of the Geneva Conventions. These include providing voluntary assistance to the medical corps of the armed forces in caring for the sick and wounded and providing assistance to prisoners of war. All the volunteers and professionals who work for the Red Cross are united by the same ideals. The men, women, and young people who volunteer for Red Cross work all seek to serve their fellowmen. People of all races, nationalities, and religious beliefs work together toward the greatest goal of the Red Cross — peace.

The three emblems of the League of Red Cross Societies.

The Ideals of the Red Cross

The laws and ideals that govern the work of the Red Cross are the heart of all its activities.

The basic laws of the Red Cross are the four Geneva Conventions. They take their name from the city in which the Red Cross was established and where the world headquarters of the Red Cross are located today. Every nation that is a member of the Red Cross has ratified the Geneva Conventions.

The four Geneva Conventions protect sick and wounded members of the armed forces on land and sea, provide regulations for the treatment of prisoners of war, and lay down the rules for the protection of civilians in time of war.

Taken together, the Geneva Conventions make up over one-half of the international law pertaining to warfare. The Geneva Conventions exist to *protect* the victims of war. They do not *govern* the laws and customs of warfare.

Wherever there is a Red Cross society, the members are also guided by seven basic principles. These seven ideals are humanity, impartiality, neutrality, independence, voluntary service, unity, and universality. Let us look at what these words mean in terms of the Red Cross.

Humanity. The purpose of the Red Cross is to ease human suffering and to encourage health and respect for all people. The Red

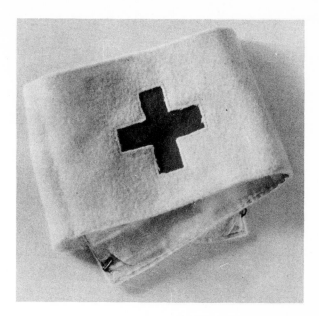

The Red Cross emblem first appeared on a battlefield on this armband, worn by Dr. Louis Appia in 1864 during the war between Prussia and Denmark.

Cross works actively for understanding, friendship, cooperation, and peace for all people.

Impartiality. The Red Cross does not discriminate, or show favor, in any way among nations, races, religions, social classes, or political ideas.

Neutrality. The Red Cross does not take sides.

Independence. Although the national societies of the Red Cross are arms of their governments that work to help people live better, they must remain independent of politics in order to uphold the Red Cross principles.

Voluntary service. The Red Cross is a voluntary organization. It does not ever work for money or gain of any kind.

Unity. A nation may have only one Red Cross society. The society must be open to everyone.

Universality. The Red Cross is a worldwide organization in which all the member societies work, share, and act as equals.

How the Red Cross Is Organized

	Governments that have signed the Geneva Conventions	
International Committee of the Red Cross	International Conference of the Red Cross (Standing Commission of the Red Cross)	League of Red Cross Societies
	National Red Cross, Red Crescent, Red Lion and Sun Societies	

You can see from the above diagram that the Red Cross has several major divisions. On a worldwide level the most important are the International Committee of the Red Cross and the League of Red Cross Societies.

Representatives of the national Red Cross societies usually meet every four years at the International Conference of the Red Cross to discuss their common problems and to plan for the future. The Standing Commission of the Red Cross sees to it that the work of all the different parts of the organization is continued between International Conferences.

The work of the International Committee of the Red Cross, the League of Red Cross Societies, and some representative national societies is described in the following pages.

10

The International Committee of the Red Cross

The International Committee of the Red Cross (ICRC) is the oldest division of the organization. It began its work in 1863, when the committee first met in Geneva to establish the Red Cross. The International Committee of the Red Cross still has its headquarters in Geneva, and its twenty-five members are all Swiss citizens.

The basic job of the ICRC is to do all it can to make sure that the four Geneva Conventions are upheld. Another activity of the committee is to encourage new nations to establish Red Cross societies. Because the committee is totally neutral it may act as a go-between in an armed conflict. Members of the committee usually are permitted to inspect prisoner-of-war camps. They act to make sure that the prisoners are well treated, and they handle mail and food packages for prisoners. The committee may also work to rescue people who have been trapped when armed conflict breaks out and to provide emergency relief for refugees fleeing a war zone.

The greatest test for the ICRC came during World War II. Between 1939 and 1945, delegates from the committee made 11,000 inspection tours of prisoner-of-war camps. The reports on the conditions in the camp were given to the governments that ran the camps and to the countries from which the prisoners came. As a result, camp conditions often were improved. During the war the ICRC helped deliver about 36 million packages of food and other goods to about 3 million prisoners behind the barbed wire that fenced the camps.

Some of the most dramatic work of the ICRC is done by the Central Tracing Agency, which helps to locate people who were separated from their families by the upheavals of the war. The heart of the agency's effort to reunite people is its index of nearly 50 million cards. Each year the agency receives about 50,000 requests for help in finding a lost relative or friend. The agency is able to provide information in about 30 percent of the cases.

The Central Tracing Agency's files are checked and cross-checked to find the needed information. The cards in the index contain painstakingly collected information. The sources range from such obvious ones as prisoner-of-war lists to names scrawled on smudged scraps of paper that somehow arrive at the agency. Once a list of names of prisoners who were being deported from the Balkans was written on a package of cigarettes. The package was thrown from a train window and picked up. Almost miraculously, it reached the agency in Geneva.

In addition to collecting information, the agency must judge carefully how to file it. Lists of names arrive at the agency in every language, every kind of writing, and with every kind of misspelling. Then there is the problem of people with similar last names, and even similar first and last names. For example, in the German part of the card index about 50,000 Müllers share the first name Hans. As a result, the agency must collect as much information about each case as it can. This may include such obvious facts as a birth date and less obvious and harder-to-learn details such as a man's last-known employer.

Here, in the words of the Central Tracing Agency is how a successful search worked.

Headquarters in Geneva, Switzerland, of the International Committee of the Red Cross.

A Polish worker, Henrik G., born in Germany, settled in his country of origin in 1938; he was captured during the war and forced to fight in the German army. Thanks to the Red Cross, his wife succeeded in finding him in Poland and wrote to him in 1944, but then lost trace of him again. He was heard of in 1949; he had been a prisoner in France and had worked on a farm somewhere west of Paris. In 1958, the Red Cross received a request from his children, then settled in South America, to undertake further inquiries.

13

The Agency got in touch with his last-known employer, who himself expressed the wish to receive news of his former worker. The inquiry continued in various other *departements* in the west of France as well as through the German Red Cross, which finally succeeded in discovering his address. As the South American Red Cross Society responsible for forwarding the results of the inquiry wrote to the Agency: "It is easy to imagine the joy of the missing man's wife and children, who had been without news of him for over twenty years."

"Henrik G." is only one of millions of people who have been helped by the ICRC. In recent years the committee has continued to serve a troubled world. While children starved in Biafra, which had seceded from the African nation of Nigeria in 1967, delegates from the ICRC worked to convince authorities on both sides to allow emergency shipments of foods and medical supplies to be delivered. In North Vietnam the ICRC asked to inspect prisoner-of-war camps. The Hanoi government refused, saying that since there was no declared war the captured American flyers were criminals, not prisoners of war. Since the ICRC is neutral it cannot condemn a government but must try to persuade it to act humanely. During the long civil war in Yemen, Arabia, in the early 1960's, two Red Cross physicians made a long and dangerous trip to persuade both sides to accept the Geneva Conventions. They succeeded, and victims of the struggle began to receive the medical and relief supplies they needed.

The worldwide efforts of the International Committee of the Red Cross are supported in many different ways by the national Red Cross societies and by the League that unites the work of the societies.

Biafran refugees go to get food at a feeding center run by the International Committee of the Red Cross.

This American Red Cross recruitment poster from World War I includes a picture of President Woodrow Wilson.

The League of
Red Cross Societies

In 1917, during World War I, United States President Woodrow Wilson appointed Henry P. Davison as chairman of the American Red Cross War Council. Davison's first job was to supervise the $330 million relief program of the American Red Cross in Europe. The war ended in 1918 but the chaos and misery it had caused were still tragically evident. It would take years of work, cooperation, and vast amounts of money to erase the years of bloodshed.

Davison was convinced that the national Red Cross societies could work better to help each other in times of war and disaster if they were united. Davison worked swiftly to bring his idea to life. By May, 1919, the League of Red Cross Societies was founded with five members — the United States, Great Britain, France, Italy, and Japan.

Today the League is a giant federation of the more than one hundred national societies. The League unites and directs the work of the national societies in times of need. It works also to help the Red Cross societies in the new nations of the world to develop good programs in such areas as health, hygiene, and first aid. It is the League, too, that acts as a representative and spokesman for all the Red Cross societies on the international level, as at the United Nations.

Wars, revolutions, floods, hurricanes, earthquakes, volcanic eruption, epidemics, famine — these are the man-made and natural disasters that the League works to relieve. When a national society cannot handle the relief program for a disaster on its own, it calls on the League for help. Cold numbers — 103 calamities in one decade — say little about how many people wept to see a baby die of hunger, a home flattened by a typhoon, or the work of a lifetime tumbled to dust in an earthquake. But then there are no words either to describe the remarkable speed with which the League organizes its relief programs.

On May 11, 1965, a cyclone hit the coast of East Pakistan. Thirty thousand square miles of land were affected. In addition to the thousands who were killed, there were countless people left injured or homeless. It was estimated that 5,000,000 Pakistanis needed help. The job was too large for the Pakistanis to handle alone. They asked the League for help. An appeal was sent out by the League to nations all over the world for powdered milk, water purification tablets, medicines, bandages, clothing, and cash to buy additional supplies at the scene. Forty-five national societies

Relief supplies from the League of Red Cross Societies arrive in Turkey following an earthquake in 1966.

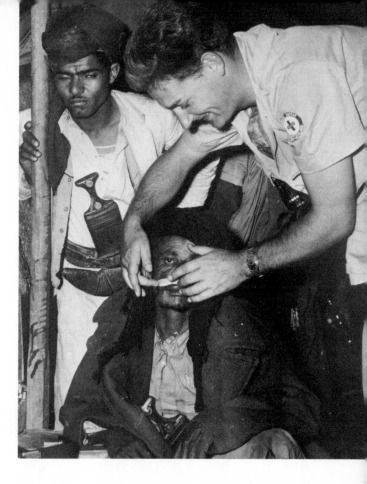

A male nurse of the Swiss Red Cross, sent by the League of Red Cross Societies to aid wounded soldiers in Yemen in 1964.

answered the call. Two relief experts were sent to Pakistan by the League to coordinate the immense work involved.

This is only one example out of hundreds and hundreds of cases that shows how the League relieves pain and suffering where it can. Again and again, the League has given the world proof that men of all races and beliefs can work together. The League not only eases pain but helps bring the world closer to permanent peace through mutual understanding and cooperation. The League's motto, *Per humanitatem ad pacem* — "Through Humanity to Peace" — perfectly sums up its work and its goals.

19

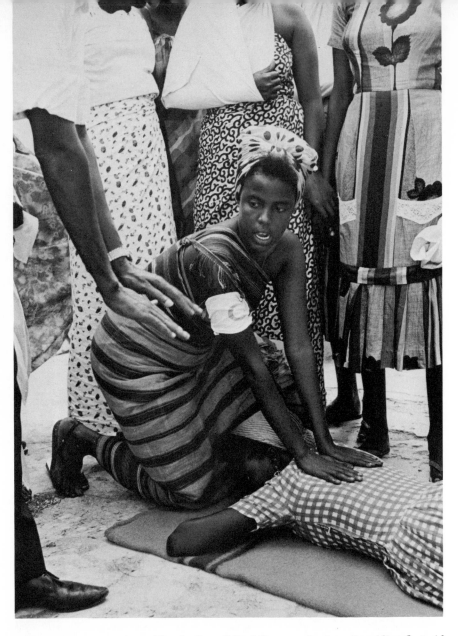

A first aid course conducted by the Somali Red Crescent Society. Providing first aid instruction is an important part of the work of national Red Cross societies.

The National Societies

It is the League of Red Cross Societies that coordinates relief in large-scale disasters, but it is the national societies that carry on the day-to-day programs of the Red Cross in their own lands. Nearly every independent country in the world has its own national society affiliated with the League. *Rotes Kreuz, Cruz Roja, Croce Rossa, Cruz Vermelha* — or something harder to say — the names all mean Red Cross in different languages and all are prepared to help in time of need.

The *basic* job of each Red Cross national society is exactly the same as Dunant had in mind when he suggested that the Red Cross be established. Each society recruits and trains volunteers who can serve as aides to the military medical branch of their government. A national Red Cross society may also produce such goods as bandages and clothing that are used in the care and treatment of the wounded. A government may also request that a national Red Cross society help care for the sick and the wounded in wartime by organizing, training, equipping, and maintaining ambulance services, and field and base hospitals.

From the beginning of its history, it has been clear that the Red Cross was prepared to relieve natural disasters just as it did the suffering of war victims. One of the first national societies to use its volunteer manpower and resources for the relief of a natural dis-

21

aster was the American Red Cross. Today many Red Cross societies are active in programs of disaster preparedness and disaster relief.

Since the League of Red Cross Societies was established in 1919 numerous societies have also been active in the field of health. The Red Cross in every country teaches people how to protect and improve their health. The enormous field of health includes first aid instruction, the prevention of disease, blood transfusion, the care

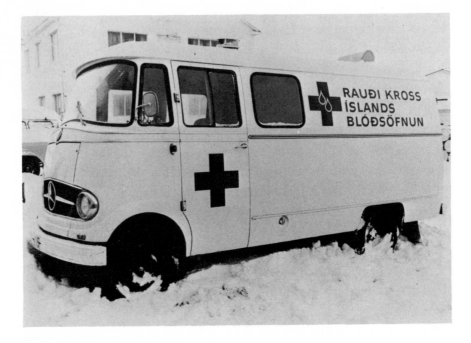

Among other things, national Red Cross societies maintain ambulance services. The ambulance in this picture belongs to the Icelandic Red Cross.

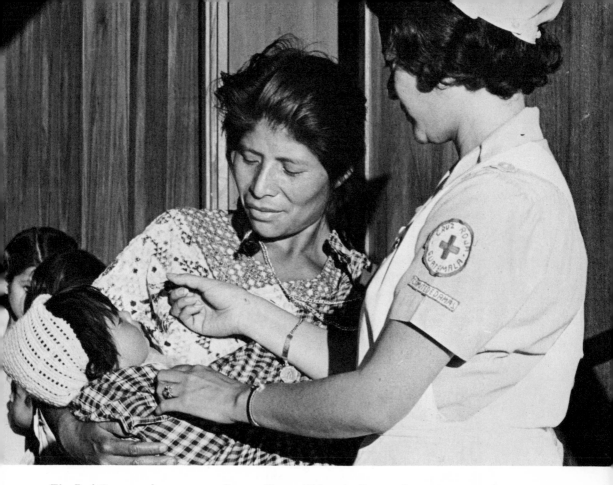

The Red Cross works to prevent disease. Here, children in Guatemala receive anti-poliomyelitis vaccine.

of mothers and children, a broad program of social work, and nurses' training.

First aid instruction teaches volunteers the simple, precise methods of treatment that can be applied when an accident or sudden illness occurs. First aid is not meant to be a substitute for a doctor's care. It is emergency treatment given to make the patient more

23

comfortable and to increase his chances of survival until the doctor arrives. Young people and adults who have taken first aid courses are trained to deal with a variety of emergencies ranging from sunstroke to drowning. Volunteers who have won first aid certificates may join first aid teams that are called into action in time of disaster or for such specific purposes as working as part of a water safety team, in highway first aid, and first aid in places of work. In some countries the Red Cross also provides first aid training for members of police forces and fire departments, and for others who work with large numbers of people.

The Red Cross is as interested in preventing disease and accidents as it is in relieving them when they do occur. Many national programs teach good health habits and safety. Others train volunteers to care for the sick, for the elderly and the chronically ill, and for mothers with newborn babies.

With the growth of the world's population there has come an increase in accidents and the need for lifesaving blood transfusions. In Australia, Belgium, Canada, Finland, Indonesia, the Republic of Korea, the Philippines, Switzerland, the Netherlands, and Turkey the Red Cross runs the national blood program, which includes the collection, preparation, and distribution of blood for transfusion. In other countries the Red Cross acts to inform the public of the need for blood donations; it sometimes recruits donors as well.

In many national societies the Red Cross directs social work programs. These may be limited to acting as a go-between for individuals trying to obtain service and the organizations that give service. Special programs have also been developed by some national societies to provide for the needs of the handicapped and the elderly. The American Red Cross also developed programs such as REACH in which traditional Red Cross programs such as first aid

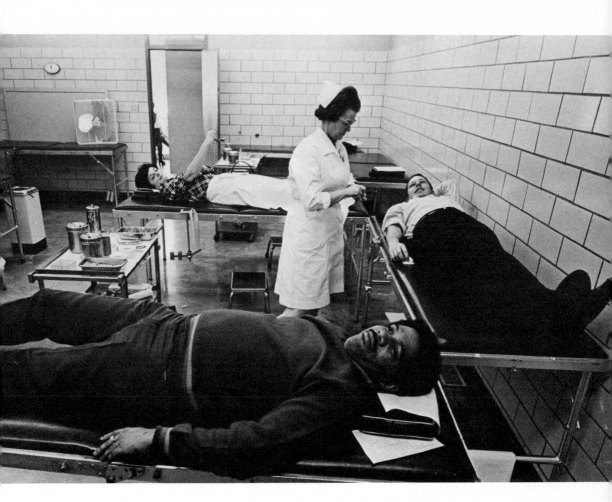

A regional blood center in North Carolina, run by the American Red Cross.

and water safety served as a bridge to the poorer members of a community.

Nurses' training is an important part of Red Cross work in many nations. Red Cross nurses may work with their army's medical services as technical advisers in nursing or as teachers of other nurses and aides. Nurses with many Red Cross societies act as instructors in public health education programs and also provide social welfare and disaster relief when needed.

Red Cross programs vary from nation to nation so that the people of each country are served in the best possible way. The programs are flexible because each nation has different problems and different needs. The Red Cross exists to meet those needs.

How a New Red Cross Society
Begins Its Work

Just after World War II ended there were about 65 national Red Cross, Red Crescent, and Red Lion and Sun Societies in the world. By 1970 that number had reached 112. Many of the new national societies were formed in emerging countries in Asia and Africa. These newer societies often have special problems and special needs. Often the country in which the young society is located has few resources. There may be only a small number of trained people to help start the Red Cross programs. Funds for the programs are usually limited. However, the health problems that must be solved are often serious and require large numbers of people and huge sums of money.

To meet some of the problems of the newer societies and to expand the work of older societies, the Red Cross Development Program was started by the League of Red Cross Societies in the 1960's. The first step of the League is, of course, to encourage the new nation to establish a Red Cross society. The new society is helped by the League and all its member nations to provide the whole range of Red Cross services.

In almost all of the newer Red Cross societies there are urgent problems to solve with all kinds of obstacles to overcome, from widespread ignorance of the Red Cross goals to a shortage of

A Red Cross worker in Kenya demonstrates the proper procedure for bathing a baby. The Mobile Health Education Unit of the Kenya Red Cross visits different parts of the country.

trained leaders and technical resources. The first step is to train a group of volunteer leaders who in turn will train the entire population. Often the first Red Cross course is in first aid. Soon afterward other programs are launched — from health education to mother and child care.

Special problems must be considered in each country. What kind of hospitals exist and are they well supplied? Are there special safety problems to be confronted on the beaches, along the rivers, or on the highways? Are there any services for the handicapped? Is the country frequently affected by natural disasters such as earthquakes and typhoons?

As these questions are answered a program can be tailored to the new society's needs. The League also encourages older societies to provide trained assistance and financial help to the new societies. Advisers and technical experts visit the new national society to help train local volunteers and to set up effective programs. Leaders from the new national societies are also invited to attend international seminars run by the League to increase their knowledge. Volunteers from a young society also make study visits to older societies to learn how they operate.

In the first three years of its existence the Red Cross in Upper Volta in Africa showed just how rapidly and effectively a new society can become a vital part of its nation's life. The organization's first program was in first aid because many people lived in areas far removed from medical help. The first aid courses were also used to teach basic hygiene and health habits. A plan was drawn up to provide first aid posts along a highway where there were frequent serious accidents on overcrowded buses. Programs were also set up to provide relief parcels of food and clothing for the old and the poor.

Persons displaced by war in Cambodia in 1970 receive assistance from the Red Cross.

The newer national Red Cross societies are growing rapidly because they help to serve vital human needs that were long neglected. The members of the younger societies can look with pride at how much they have accomplished in a short time and with gratitude to the technical and financial assistance provided through the League. The future is brighter for many nations because Red Cross services are now available to them.

Clara Barton and the American National Red Cross

Today the American National Red Cross is one of the largest national societies in the League of Red Cross Societies. Its story started on the battlefields of the Civil War when a former schoolteacher named Clara Barton helped provide relief for the wounded in both the Union and Confederate armies.

Clara Barton was born in North Oxford, Massachusetts, on Christmas Day, 1821. Clara was a small, plain child, who distinguished herself by learning how to spell before she went to school. As she grew up, it was obvious that she would not be able to work in the textile mills like her older brothers and sisters because she was too short to reach the spindles. It was decided that Clara would become a schoolteacher.

Between 1839 and 1854 Clara taught in one school after another. Often her students were bigger and stronger than she was, but the tiny woman was a firm and good teacher who knew how to keep her classes interested. Then, suddenly, Clara Barton fell ill with throat trouble. Her teaching career was over. She took a job at the United States Patent Office in Washington, D.C. She was working there when the Civil War began in April, 1861.

The hardworking clerk was transformed almost overnight into a dedicated volunteer. She saw how badly the soldiers needed help with such things as reading and writing letters. When the first wounded men were brought to the capital city, it was Clara Barton who helped organize emergency relief. She gathered blankets, clothing, food, and bandages and helped to distribute them.

Only two years had passed since 1859, when Jean Henri Dunant had aided the victims of the Battle of Solferino. Now Clara Barton was also determined to go to the actual battlefields. She told all the high officials she could reach that if they would give her the necessary pass, she would take relief supplies to the field hospitals. It was not easy to convince the military men to let a woman do this work. But she persisted, reminding each listener that she had gathered the needed supplies herself from friends in Massachusetts. And, after all, she told the officers, more than forty of the men in one Union division were her former pupils.

Clara Barton's determination won her the pass. In the summer of 1862 she arrived at the front with a four-mule-team wagonload of supplies. The field hospital she reached was nearly out of surgical dressings. The army surgeon wrote that Clara Barton made him think "that night if heaven ever sent out a holy angel, she must be the one, her assistance was so timely." Throughout the war years, and afterward, the hardworking Miss Barton was known everywhere as "the Angel of the Battlefield." At Cedar Mountain, Bullrun, Antietam, Fredericksburg, and during the Wilderness Campaign, Miss Barton served wounded men and prisoners of both Union and Confederate armies. And so it went as long as she was needed. Clara drove herself hard. She never let fear or fatigue stop her.

Near the end of the war, as news of her work spread, families began to write her for information about their missing sons. Miss Barton realized another human need had to be met. Everything

Clara Barton, founder of the American Red Cross, in a photograph by Matthew Brady, one of America's most famous photographers.

possible would have to be done to identify the unknown dead. It was a grim and terrible job, but Clara Barton insisted that it be done. A month before he died, President Abraham Lincoln issued this appeal:

To the friends of missing persons: Miss Clara Barton has kindly offered to search for the missing prisoners of war. Please address her at Annapolis, giving her name, regiment and company of any missing prisoner.

Clara Barton's enormous job was a sad one. By 1869, Miss Barton could report that she had been able to provide information concerning the fate of more than 20,000 men. Today, the job of tracing those lost in war is one of the main activities of the International Committee of the Red Cross. It was Clara Barton who began the job in the United States.

By the end of the war "the Angel of the Battlefield" was known throughout the nation. She was also exhausted from her years of service to both armies. In 1869 she went to Europe to rest. She was in Geneva when the Franco-Prussian War began in 1870. Miss Barton was invited to join the volunteers of the International Committee of the Red Cross. She wore a red ribbon in the shape of the cross as her identification. Clara Barton helped distribute relief supplies in several cities and set up workrooms where the civilian victims of war could make badly needed clothing. Today, in some countries the distribution of clothing to war and disaster victims is still an important Red Cross activity. Clara Barton had anticipated another need the organization was to fill.

The officials of the International Red Cross in Geneva saw that Clara Barton was the ideal person to establish the Red Cross in the

A poster depicting Clara Barton at work at Antietam during the Civil War.

United States. They chose well. Only a person as determined as she was would have kept on trying to persuade the United States government in spite of so many obstacles.

In 1877, President Rutherford B. Hayes flatly refused to let the United States become involved in "entangling alliances" with foreign countries. But in 1881, President James Garfield seemed ready to sign the Geneva Convention. On July 2, 1881, President Garfield was fatally shot by an assassin. One result of that tragedy was

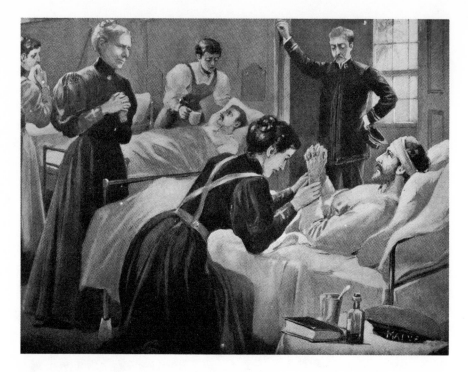

An artist's conception of Clara Barton directing relief operations during the Spanish-American War.

that still another president and still more advisers had to be persuaded of the importance of the Red Cross in the United States.

In the same year — 1881 — forest fires raged in Michigan. Miss Barton's newly formed American Association of the Red Cross raised $80,000 to provide relief supplies to the hundreds of families that were left homeless. This one event showed that the Red Cross could provide its greatly needed services to victims of peacetime disasters, just as it did in war. The Red Cross had added still another branch to its services under Clara Barton's direction.

Finally, in 1882, the Congress of the United States ratified the

Geneva Treaty. For the next twenty-two years Clara Barton guided the work of the Red Cross. When floods on the Mississippi and Ohio rivers left thousands of families homeless in 1884, the Red Cross raised funds and distributed the needed supplies to small, isolated communities, under Miss Barton's personal direction.

In 1889 a terrible flood almost erased Johnstown, Pennsylvania, a town of thirty thousand. Over two thousand people were killed. The survivors had to rebuild their town and their lives. The Red Cross was on the scene within five days of the disaster. It remained for five months. When a hurricane hit the Sea Islands off the South Carolina coast in 1893, the Red Cross was the only organization that could help. For ten months it worked with the survivors of that disaster.

The list is endless, for the American Red Cross from Miss Barton's day to this has gone to help wherever the need arose, even abroad. In 1892, relief was organized for famine victims in Russia. Then in 1896, when war broke out between the Turks and the Armenians, the American Red Cross, under Miss Barton's personal guidance, helped distribute money, medicine, food, and farm tools. Only two years later, in 1898, the remarkable woman of seventy-six was on her way to Cuba to direct relief operations during the Spanish-American War.

The tradition of serving the wounded of war and victims of peacetime disasters was a firm part of the American Red Cross tradition when Miss Barton resigned as its president in 1904. The "one real, true representative of the Red Cross in this country," as a newspaper called Clara Barton, died in 1912. Her years of service to her country and to the world are part of the strong fabric that has made the Red Cross the world's most important charitable organization.

The American Red Cross
in Action

The American Red Cross now has about 3,300 chapters in 50 states. Over 2,000,000 volunteers work to carry out the many different Red Cross programs. On the local, state, and federal levels the American Red Cross is directed by volunteers. Nearly all of its duties are performed by volunteers; all its work is financed by voluntary contributions.

Under its charter from Congress, the American Red Cross is to serve members of the armed forces and their families. It is also required by law to direct a system of national and international relief to prevent and ease the suffering caused by disasters.

In addition, the Red Cross collects and processes blood from volunteer donors. The Red Cross has a group of trained nurses who are prepared to serve in emergencies. Among the best-known training programs of the American Red Cross are those for volunteers. These trained volunteers serve in Red Cross chapters, hospitals, clinics, and other agencies. The Red Cross also provides mobile units and first aid stations for highways. Other well-known training programs are those in home nursing, first aid, and water safety.

The Red Cross water safety program was launched in 1914 by Wilbert E. Longfellow, a former newspaperman who described himself as "an amiable whale." His ambition was to "waterproof

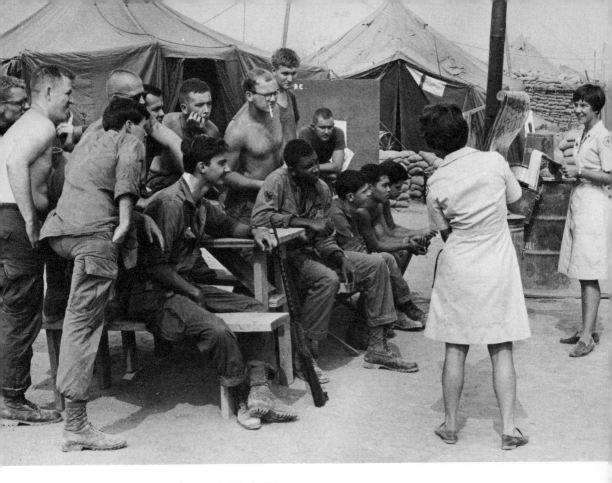

American Red Cross workers and GI's in Vietnam.

America." Longfellow started the Red Cross Life Saving Corps by gathering the best swimmers in a town to teach them lifesaving skills. This group was then ready to supervise swimming activities in the town. The next step was for the trained lifesavers to give widespread swimming instruction. The Red Cross Water Safety Program has grown with each passing year and with it the number of swimming accidents has gone down. Each step on the road from

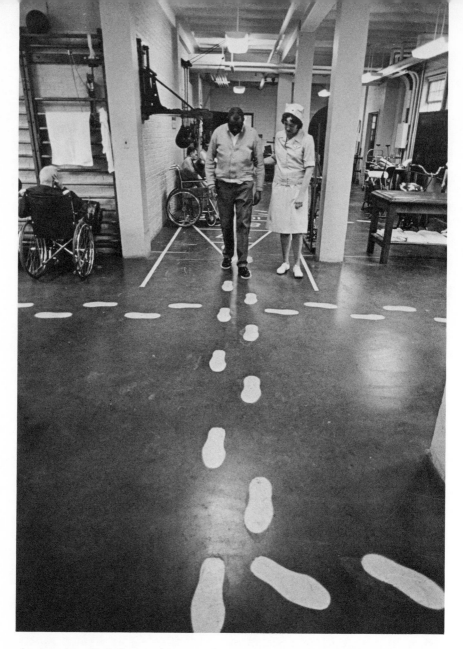

An American Red Cross volunteer helps with physical therapy exercises in a Veterans' Administration hospital.

a Beginner's swimming certificate to Senior Life Saver is a milestone in safe fun for millions of young swimmers.

It is clear that by the beginning of World War I the Red Cross in the United States was serving Americans in many different ways. But everything that went before was overshadowed by the war effort. During the war the Red Cross set up and staffed 54 base hospitals in Europe. The Red Cross provided 20,000 nurses to serve in hospitals at home and abroad. Volunteer ambulance brigades served with great bravery. Additional thousands of volunteers worked at small but vital tasks, such as making surgical dressings and knitting warm clothes for refugees. Still thousands more served coffee and doughnuts to the troops in canteens or wrote letters for bedridden servicemen in hospitals. Enormous amounts of money and goods were sent to Europe to help the civilian population recover from the terrible effects of the war. When American service-

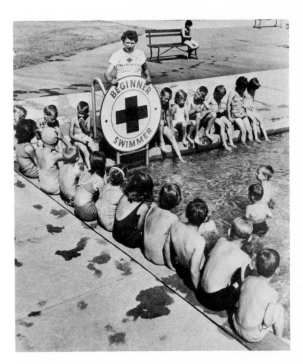

Beginners' swimming classes are conducted by the American Red Cross.

A poster asking for funds to help the American Red Cross with its work during World War II.

men came home at the end of the war, the Red Cross was there to help them and their families.

The Red Cross was soon back at its peacetime activities. Programs in home nursing, first aid, and water safety grew. One disaster after another continued to get a quick response — an earthquake in Japan, floods in the West Indies and in the United States, a drought affecting twenty-three states, and then the Great Depression of the 1930's. Then war came again and once more the American Red Cross had to turn to the battlefields.

During World War II the American Red Cross performed a variety of services. From 1941 to 1945 it ran the Army-Navy Blood Donor Service that collected 13,300,000 pints of blood. Nine hundred clubs and nearly 400 canteens and clubmobiles were established and run for servicemen by volunteer workers in places from London, England, to tiny islands in the Pacific. The Red Cross recruited and trained 212,000 nurses. And in chapters all over the country, clothing was made for servicemen, and almost 28 million food packages were prepared for war prisoners.

The figures can be piled one on top of the other, forming what might be described as a skyscraper of statistics. Behind each number is a story — a soldier whose life was saved by blood collected by the Red Cross, a prisoner to whom a food parcel was a reminder that he had not been forgotten. And behind each number is the amazing fact that by 1945 over half the adults in the United States were contributing members of the Red Cross.

Another remarkable fact is that there were no major disasters to tax the American Red Cross at home during World War II. Of course, neither disaster nor war had vanished. The decade 1950–60 has been called "the worst disaster decade in American history." Floods devastated Kansas, Missouri, Oklahoma, and Illinois in 1951 and states in the East and the West in 1955. In addition, the American Red Cross provided large-scale assistance to the refugees of the Hungarian uprising in 1956 and the survivors of the Chilean earthquakes of 1960.

The staff and volunteers of the American Red Cross met fresh challenges in the 1960's. Services to the armed forces, veterans, and families continued in Korea, Vietnam, and at other places around the globe. Specialists from the American Red Cross worked through the League to help new societies build strong health programs. The Red Cross Blood Program continued to grow and now supplies about 50 percent of the whole blood used in the United States, as well as a large percentage of blood derivatives like gamma globulin.

Two totally different kinds of disasters hit the United States in

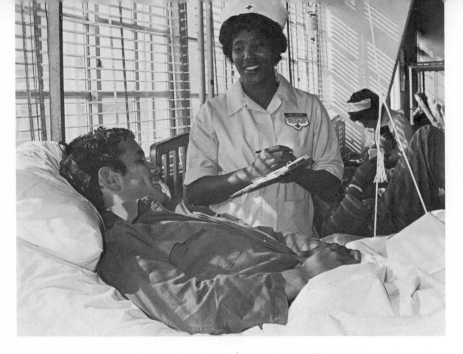

An American Red Cross volunteer in Japan helps a soldier wounded in Vietnam.

1965 and each showed that the Red Cross continued to be ready to serve wherever it was needed. The sudden, massive power failure that blacked out much of the northeastern states and parts of Canada on November 9 was one of these. Red Cross volunteers in the span of one night saved at least one life, preserved thousands of pints of blood, and cared for tens of thousands of people who could not reach their homes. Batteries were quickly provided for a man whose iron lung machine was powered by electricity. Elsewhere emergency generators were put to work to keep stored blood at the proper temperature. At air and bus terminals, railway stations, and armories the Red Cross fed the stranded. Cots and blankets were distributed at subway stations.

The well-prepared and coordinated work of that one night on

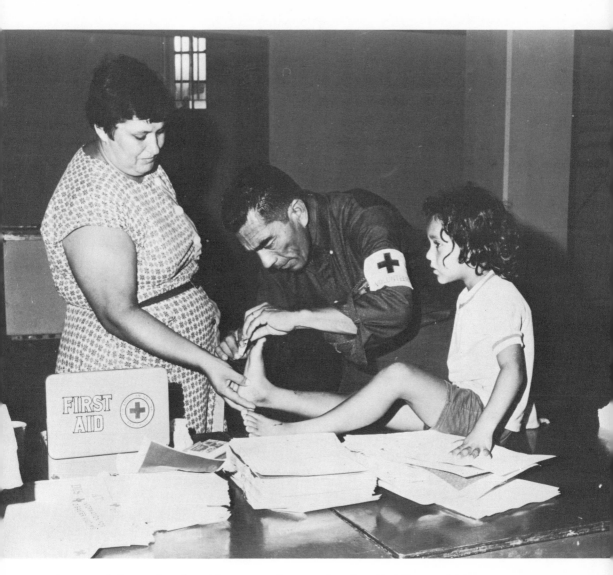

A young victim receives first aid treatment from an American Red Cross volunteer following Hurricane Celia in 1970.

American Red Cross aid helped victims of heavy floods in California in 1964.

the east coast was repeated day in and day out for months after Hurricane Betsy hit the Gulf States in September, 1965. Even before the hurricane battered homes, snapped telephone lines, and isolated whole areas the Red Cross was ready. Years of training on the local, state, and national level had prepared staff members and volunteers for disaster relief.

When the United States Weather Bureau started tracking the storm, the Red Cross began its Hurricane Watch Plan. Shelters were prepared. Mobile units called Readiness Emergency Actions Vans stood by to take food and supplies to Red Cross centers. There the vans could be used as communications centers because of their emergency generators.

When the Red Cross had time to look back on Hurricane Betsy and count, it saw that 850 national and chapter staff members from 48 states had come to help. They were assisted by 11,000 volunteers and many other agencies as well.

Hardly a day passes that the American Red Cross is not called upon to serve. Each time it responds, it brings hope to the countless victims of disaster.

Junior Red Cross volunteers in Dahomey at work on the land, following heavy rains.

Red Cross Youth

In a village in Ghana, a young man named Badu learned through work with the Junior Red Cross that flies and insects cause disease and death. He taught his family how to cover food to keep the insects off. He showed them how to bury their garbage. When the rainy season began, he made drains to lead the water away from the village. This helped eliminate a mosquito-breeding place. Because of Badu's training and his work, the high death rate in his village dropped. The villagers had learned that man could be killed by disease-carrying insects.

When severe floods hit northwestern Yugoslavia several years ago, the local Red Cross picked a primary school to serve as a reception center for flood victims. Within 24 hours, 420 people had been brought to the school. Teachers, helped by hardworking members of the Junior Red Cross, turned the school into a dormitory and canteen. Other young Red Cross volunteers brought clothing and toys for younger flood victims. Many of the young volunteers spent hours helping to dry tears and to cheer little children by playing with them.

A fifteen-year-old English girl, the member of a Junior Red Cross group in Essex, spent every Saturday shopping and doing errands for old people who were housebound. Her bright smile and useful work made her a favorite of all the shut-ins she aided.

In a small town in the Soviet Union a seventeen-year-old girl named Maria was severely burned. Only skin grafts would make it possible for her to live a normal life. But who would donate skin for Maria? When the question was put to her two hundred school-mates, all of them volunteered. One of them explained, "You see, we are Red Cross health volunteers. The protection of health is our duty." Four girls were selected as donors and Maria's operation was a complete success.

There are stories like these to be told in every Red Cross Youth organization in the world. Millions of young people have learned how to live well and usefully through their work with the Red Cross.

No one is quite sure, though, how the Junior Red Cross got started. Unofficially, the Netherlands Red Cross may claim to have

An elderly handicapped lady is helped with her Christmas shopping by two British Red Cross Juniors.

New Zealand Junior Red Cross members make toys for children's homes and hospitals.

the youth program with the oldest roots. In 1870, Dutch school-children were asked to contribute to relief for victims of the Franco-Prussian War. The formal history of Red Cross Youth starts with World War I in 1914. In that year children in New South Wales, Australia; Saskatchewan, Canada; and in the United States began to work with their national societies in large numbers. The Junior Red Cross came into official existence in 1918. In 1922 the League of Red Cross Societies urged every national society to set up a junior division. Today over 60 million young people are members of Red Cross Youth programs.

51

It is fun to make and receive Junior Red Cross friendship boxes.

You and the Red Cross

Students in schools and colleges in the United States work, study, and serve together in Red Cross Youth programs. These programs are organized through local Red Cross chapters in cooperation with the schools.

Elementary school students take part in the Junior Red Cross activities. They study safety, good health habits, and courtesy. They help their schools and themselves by conducting health and safety campaigns. Above all, they learn how to work together for the good of all people.

The Junior Red Cross contributes to world Red Cross programs in many ways. One of the most popular is the Friendship Box Program. These boxes include health and educational aids, as well as small toys. They have brightened the lives of hundreds of thousands of children all over the globe.

The money contributed by the Junior Red Cross goes to the Red Cross Youth Fund and is used only for youth activities such as the publication of the regular and Braille editions of the American Junior Red Cross *News*. Some of the funds are used to finance health and safety programs for young people in Central America, Mexico, and Puerto Rico. Red Cross Youth funds help other countries improve their programs. The money may be used to buy first aid kits for the Congo, to support a children's home in Australia, or to provide food for a needy family in Argentina.

Older students can make a real contribution to their community by working with their local Red Cross chapter. Help is always needed in a wide range of activities such as nursing, safety services, disaster training and disaster relief, fund raising, public information, and special projects that assist less fortunate young people.

For students interested in nursing, for example, the Red Cross provides courses in home nursing and for nurse's aides. After the course comes work in a hospital as an assistant to the professional medical staff. Assistants may help patients to write letters, to perform errands, or simply to pass time in friendly conversation. Other hospital jobs that Red Cross student volunteers may help with include those in the hospital pharmacy, on the clerical staff, or with the recreation director. Many homes and hospitals for the elderly and the chronically ill welcome programs and skits prepared and acted by members of Red Cross Youth.

There are many opportunities in Red Cross health and safety programs. The first step, naturally, is to learn health and safety skills. Courses are available in water safety, small-craft safety, first aid, care of the sick and injured, or mother and baby care. Such training is useful in times of emergency or if first aid teams are to be organized in a school. Volunteer safety aids are needed to help teach small children to swim and to give small-craft demonstrations. A job that is always vital is to encourage other people to learn more about the Red Cross health and safety programs and take part in them.

Another important job in the health field involves working with the Blood Donor Program. Volunteers help recruit blood donors, register donors when collections are made, and organize transportation for donors. Additional volunteers are also needed to prepare refreshments to serve the donors after they have given blood.

The Red Cross conducts many different kinds of health and safety programs. The students in this picture are demonstrating mouth-to-mouth resuscitation.

The Red Cross needs its trained volunteers not only after disaster strikes but in helping prepare programs in case disaster occurs. Volunteers can work with a local disaster planning committee, or help hold a mock disaster drill. If disaster does strike, workers will be required in communications as messengers, or if able, as ham radio operators. Mass-care operations must have help in amusing small children being cared for in shelters or in preparing food for large numbers of homeless people. Volunteers may help, also, by sorting and distributing clothing and other supplies. Other workers can help survey teams trying to measure the damage done. In addi-

Members of a youth disaster team in Texas sort clothing donated to the American Red Cross.

tion, there are displaced people that have to be found. It is also important to keep the public informed of hour-to-hour developments.

Fortunately disasters are quite rare, but there are many daily problems that volunteers in Red Cross Youth can help ease. Physically and mentally handicapped children need help. Under the guidance of a local chapter this may take the form of visits to the child's home to read to him or even helping him to learn to walk or swim.

There is also work to be done with educationally and emotionally disadvantaged children. The Red Cross may help by providing them with tutoring services or assisting on outings to places of interest, such as zoos and museums.

The Red Cross in any community can suggest many other ways that volunteer services can be of use. There is often important work for young people to do in fund raising, public information, and service to military families. In cooperation with a local school, there is work to be done helping to prepare chests of health and educational supplies for schools in other countries. Volunteers can develop TAKITS — teaching aid kits — for use in health and safety courses elsewhere in the United States or abroad.

There are many challenging adventures in the Red Cross Youth programs. Your Red Cross chapter can help you find out how you can help your community.

The Red Cross Works for Peace

The Red Cross was born on a battlefield· but it works for peace. In *A Memory of Solferino* Jean Henri Dunant wrote that "To encourage the idea of solidarity among nations in doing good is to oppose war." Dunant's words have, as you have seen, given birth to the worldwide Red Cross movement in which people of every race and every religion are united in serving each other in time of need. The Red Cross long ago grew beyond being simply a war relief agency. It is now dedicated in word and deed to bringing peace to the world.

The efforts of the Red Cross to promote international understanding and peace have won worldwide recognition. In 1946, the General Assembly of the United Nations unanimously voted to encourage member states to approve the formation of national Red Cross and Red Crescent societies because the Red Cross made "a positive contribution to the understanding and peace among nations."

On four different occasions, the Red Cross has been awarded the Nobel Peace Prize, which is given "To the person or persons who shall have done the most to promote brotherhood among nations. . . ." In 1901 when the Nobel Peace Prize was given for the first time, it was shared by Dunant, the father of the Red Cross, and Frédéric Passy, a French pacifist. The only Peace Prize awarded during World War I was given to the International Committee of the Red Cross. The honor was repeated in 1944 as a tribute to the ICRC's tireless work in World War II. In 1963 — the year the Red Cross celebrated its 100th anniversary — the Nobel Peace Prize was awarded jointly to the International Committee of the Red Cross and the League of Red Cross Societies.

At the Twentieth International Conference of the Red Cross in 1965 a resolution was passed appealing to all governments to reach an agreement banning nuclear weapons manufacture and tests, and urging a program of general disarmament. The resolution also asked the International Committee of the Red Cross to work with the United Nations in an effort to prevent and settle the disagreements that might lead to armed conflicts.

The Red Cross has grown with the changing needs of the world that it serves, but nothing it has ever attempted before equals its greatest challenge — bringing permanent peace to mankind.

Index

63